"My Thoughts From Within"

Richard B Cooper

Dedication

There are so many people that have pushed me over the years. From just writing poetry to stage plays. Friends who have read so many things on my behalf, just so I could get feedback from them. So many have inspired me to put my thoughts in book form, but like so many others I was reluctant to step out of my comfort zone.

To believe in myself. Well, I finally pushed myself out of my comfort zone, and combined just a few of my writings to give you "My Thoughts From Within"

These are a few words that some of you may be afraid to say, but I am not.

Enjoy your trip through what I see others wanting to say, but won't, so I said it for them.

I hereby dedicate this book to all my children.

Porche', Richard II, Ty'era, Tarrence, Taliya

and my Grandson Zahair

CONTENTS

About the Author

Richard was born in Houston, Texas. He is a proud product of "Third Ward High" Jack Yates Senior High School .c/o '84. He attended Lamar University and has a Bachelor of Liberal Arts and Biblical Counseling with a minor in Global Travel. Richard is a person who loves to write and will write about anything. He has written, produced, and directed many stage plays over the years and now he has unleashed a new venture. This is the first of three books that will be released. The first is this poem book with two novels to follow in 2025.

Preface

I'm forever changing, day by day—
From love to hurt, then feeling some type of way.
One day, I don't care about the world;
The next, I do.
One day, I want to cuddle;
The next, just simply f... you.

I've been through so much—ups and downs,
High as the sky, lower than the ground.
I've been spun around, blown like a tree in the wind.
It's easy to say: here are my thoughts from within.

Moments in life make or break us,
Trials we sometimes overcome,
Journeys sometimes evade us,
Many victories we haven't even won.

Sometimes we're so afraid that one day we may finally win,
That we forget to verbalize our thoughts from within.

So today it changes; today it becomes brand new.
Today, this is all about me and you—
Things you wish you would have said, but I do.

Your inner feelings, your bold mind,
Your heart, your time,

Your soul and your body,
Being in love, then being a lil' naughty.

Take a moment, so now we both can win.
Welcome to My Thoughts from Within.

Poems

Black Rose

Roses are red
Violets are blue
Hell you know the rest
But it ain't got shit to do with you.

You're elegant and beautiful by design
Not to mention you're so damn fine
Got me sucking my own finger after making love
Cause you once again blew my mind.

You're a Black Rose can't you see
If you were not, you damn sure wouldn't be with me
Shining so bright with a few drops of dew
Swaying in the wind, waiting for me to pick you.

Just picking you will not do
Cutting your stem will ruin you
So instead, I dig you deep from the root
Being careful not to bruise or break any part of you.

I rush you home and in my garden you lay
As I plant you deep, I see you start to sway
Moving your body from side to side
Hypnotizing me, damn I'm memorized.

Roses may be red
And violets may be blue
I've got a fine Black Rose
And girl, it's you.

A Rose

A rose it is just a rose like everyone thinks and
knows,
It is a rose with pedals that are closed, but when
they open,
Opens new avenues to your soul.

Made of different colors, smells and designs,
Often with long stems,
But the short ones are Devine.

Silky and smooth to the touch,
Long thorns, but they make you love them so
much.
Bunches and bunches and bunches fill a room,
Changing your moods from sad, angry and
glum.

Sometimes making it better to get through a
day,
Yet not always being that one rose that will
brighten up your day.

A rose is not just a rose when it's a Black Rose.
Now a Black Rose will give you new life and kill
your soul,

If you do not reach out and take a hold
And maintain control,
So, it does not consume your soul.

Never cutting it down or clipping its stem, only
pulling off the loose pedals to give it a trim.

Black as can be with a glow all its own,
Always satisfied where it blooms, never in search for a
new home.

The soil where it resides is its
home.

A rose isn't a rose like everyone thinks
and knows,
Yet a rose is a rose only once it
captivates your soul.

A Work In Progress

You say you want this and you want that,
But what do you have to give me back?
Please say it ain't sex, and that it's good,
He'll I can get pussy when I can't get no food.

What will it take for you to understand the type of man you
got?
Is it when my displays of love and affection stop?
What will it take that you can't see
For me to simply stop being me?

I love in a different way,
I aim to show differently each and every day.
I love ways that are not the norm,
A way that will never cause your heart any harm.

I know you're not use to being shown that you're loved,
Even when you have someone sent from high above.
Being loved should be a blessing,
Not turning someone away, them feeling like this was one of
life's lessons.

Stop being all in your feelings, thinking only of yourself,
It's making me feel like I need to be somewhere else.
When you love someone you forget about how you feel,
Give all of you that you have, in spite of, to show your love
too is real.

Be true to the one that loves you giving all of you to just him,
So that he doesn't feel he's always under a test.
It's so easy to give yourself to someone else when you feel like
you're not getting your way,
When this man loves you more than any man could all day
every day.

A

A moment to share
A moment to wish
A moment to dream
A moment of your sweet lips

A second to imagine
A second to desire
A second to reflex
A second to remind myself how you set my soul on fire

A minute to stare
A minute to see
A minute to embrace
A minute to think of what you do to me

A hour to seek
A hour to speak
A hour of silence
A hour to wonder why my mind is so weak

A day to walk
A day to run
A day to realize
A day to know with you my life has just begun

A month to be blind
A month to see
A month to establish
A month to ponder how good you are for me

A moment in time turns into a second
A second in time turns into a minute
A minute in time turns into an hour
A hour in time turns into a day
A day in time turns into a month
A month in time turns into a year
A year in time turns into how I want to love you
A time that is FOREVER!!!!!

Ain't It Funny

Hello baby, how you been?
It's nice to see your face again!
I remember when you were around,
But then it's funny how you put me down.

I was so much into you,
Remember all the things we used to do?
Remember how things were, okay?
You thought you could do better, so you went on
your way.

You thought what we had was so untrue,
But for me all I thought of was you.
I spent so many years chasing after you,
All I got was my feelings turned blue.

I wiped my tears and said that it's okay,
I picked myself up and went on my way.
You would pop up from time to time,
Then there I go again wishing you were mine.

You call and I fall,
We talk for days, then when I call, you don't answer,
And I find myself beating my head against the wall.

*You act like you want me, and I have wanted
you for so long,
Then it winds up being the same ole sad song.*

What is it with you?

*You know how I feel, my feelings have always
been true for you.
I didn't care if you were with someone else,
Just tell me the truth so I don't feel like I hate
myself.*

*For just sitting and waiting for you like I always
do,
Then once again the hurt begins to come
through.
You with someone else or even me too,
I didn't care as long I could express my love
and feelings to you.*

*You kick me to the curb then expect me to
respond to you when you text or call.
Really? To what get my feelings hurt once
again, through it all?
Knowing I have truly loved you this long.*

*My heart is no joke in which you may think,
That's why I feel like I feel now...
LOVE STINKS!*

So, forgive me for not responding the way you
think I should,
I don't want to face disappointment once again,
and I know I would.
Just hearing your voice or seeing a picture you,
Would knock me off a cliff, as they always do.

So don't tell me you get the message, when I
Haven't heard from you in months maybe even
a year nearly.
I hope all is well and you are okay,
I hope things in your life are going your way.

So, hello baby, how you been?
It was nice to hear
from you again.

All Eyes to See

I see you showing off your body for the whole world to see,
Here my dumb ass was thinking all that was for me.

I see you have them posted on Facebook, TikTok and
Instagram,
Posing, looking back at your ass like it's a big piece of ham.
All these mofos in your inbox trying to get up in that Crack,
You gone fool around and get some shit that yo ass can't give
back.

You think these dudes give a fuck about you,
They already seen what you working with,
They just want to see what other tricks you can do.

Here I am loving you and wanting to be apart of your life,
I guess it's true what they say " You can't make a HOE a
house wife.

I seen pictures of you on another dude's phone that doesn't
know I know you,
According to him, you're just someone he hits when he has
nothing else to do.
Funny thing is when I brought it to your attention,
It didn't phase you.
You just act like, oh well, and went on doing what you do.

*Well, now I can't be with you 'cause I don't know what yo
pussy been through.
You expect me to be with a woman that means the world to
me,
Yet walks around with a pussy that I can't eat.*

*My woman, my pride and joy,
From the looks of it, others' play toy.
I'ma take a step back which will be a major sacrifice,
Nothing against you, just protecting my life.*

*Not from you,
But ain't no telling what these other
motherfuckers will do behind you.
Knowing you may have turned a trick or two.
So, keep on taking pictures and posting for the world to see,
I'll just have to remember they were not just for me.*

Being Number One

You make number one who you want number one,
It shouldn't be a choice; I should be number one.

I really don't care about things in the past,
I thought I was your future, scared will it last.
I wish you talk to me, the way you talk to them,
As if they were your everything, not me them.

You make them first as if they're there day in and day out,
Yet I'm the last to know between us, yet it comes out of your
mouth.
You tell me you told them as if I'm not here,
Oh, I forgot, I just me, not them.

You may not care about them as you tell me,
Yet when I tell you how I feel, when it comes to them, you
never agree.
It's like you keeping a secret that you don't want to tell,
You're hiding it in your heart, for them it shows very well.

Why am I always the last to know?
Yet I'm always the first to show.
I give and give, but for them, I'm neglected,
You make it obvious at times; even with them, I'm not
respected.

How can I be that man if I can't be number one?
Your words say one thing, but it appears they must be your choice.
Why give of myself, so much as I do,
When I could never be that man when it's all about you.

My opinion only counts when it comes to bills around the house,
I feel like I could be replaced at the stroke of your mouse.
You care about their feeling more than you do mine,
It didn't just start, it's happens all the time.

I guess my being second, is my number one,
I guess being respected will never get done.
So much of me want to run and hide,
Yet I push and push and swallow my pride.
Keep making me feel like I'm not number one,
I'm going to ignore my pride and find a way to run.
I mentioned to you before, about the way that you do,
My words have no meaning, you show me over and over again, and yes it's true.

I'm sure I'll be second in a lot of things that I do,
But I should never be second when it comes to our family and you.
So, continue to put me second on your big list,
So, I can slowly erase the man I have become to the man I used to wish.

Don't just do it for me, do it for you,
Cause if I'm not made number one,
I'll disappear as number two.

Breathing

I didn't know what breathing was like until I met you,
Drowning in the deep waters of life, fighting waters with no
clue

Of how to keep from falling deeper, just hopeless not knowing
what to do.

It was your eyes, that guided me from the depths to the shore,
For its your eyes daily that keeps me from drowning once
more.

Trapped in my own sorrow, desperately seeking an end,
Wanting to end it all, but knowing that's a sin,
Begging myself to push, with no strength let within.

Thoughts fading fast, breathing at this rate won't last,
Afraid to open my eyes, for visions of my past,
Afraid to see my failures, Afraid of the end,
Yet one look into your eyes, calms my within,
Allowing me to see just how much I stand to win.

Breathing has become a struggle, the tide is going out,
I'm screaming as loud as I can,
But nothing comes out of my mouth.
I since again me losing myself,
Wanting it all to end, can't think of nothing else,
Then the whisper of your voice as you call out my name,

Paints a picture for me that things will never be the same.

A single touch of a fingertip, breaks all things untrue,
I never knew what breathing was, until the day that I met
you.

Can You Handle It

You would not know what to do with me if I was
lying next to you,
Holding you and caressing you, squeezing you
through and through.

Waking up in the middle of the night just to rub
your feet,
Listening to you moan in your sleep,
Making your body weak.

Staring at you watching your eyes,
They rolling around like marbles, all kinds of
thoughts in your mind,
Trying to open your eyes, but you cannot, now
you feel blind.

You are screaming loud, out of pleasure and pain,
Yelling and screaming calling out my name.
Babe Babe what are you doing to me,
Screaming so loud trying to push it out,
Yet not a sound is coming out of your mouth.

Then the touch goes to your legs, and you turn to comply,
Still in a daze, trying to figure out why.
The touch goes to your stomach, and it stays for awhile,

Up and down, Up and down,
Moving slowly side to side.

It reaches your neck and then your head,
Not staying long, cause its back to your feet so I
can go to bed.
You lay there staring into space,
No sound just moaning, oh my, the look on your face.

You want to close your eyes and fall back asleep,
You can't, you can't even move,

Your body is too weak,
You want to touch me but I'm out of your reach.
You hear a slight snore, yes that's me, I'm asleep.

It's hard to imagine what happened in the end,
Yet like I said you wouldn't know what to do
lying next to me,
Cause tomorrow it's going to happen all over
again.

Change

I go to sleep crying
I woke up with tears still in my eyes

If I could work from home
I would never go back outside

I'm afraid to face the world
Knowing that I have got to change
When at times I can't remember my own damn name

I can't look in the mirror
I don't like who I see
Don't know who it is
It damn show ain't me

Feelings

Your feelings are something,
They've yet to be seen.
Maybe your feelings are trapped deep inside your dreams.

You say you care,
Maybe you do, maybe you don't
I tell you what I need and desire,
You can, but you won't.

You're trapped inside your emotions or detached as it seems,
Maybe you're blinded by your emotions;
cause you think is a damn dream.
It appears you have put your feelings high on a shelf,
Guess I need to pack up my love
and my heart and take them somewhere else.

You know your feelings are not what they seem; if they were
we'd be on the same team.
Yet you make me feel like my feelings are just a damn dream.
Don't get me wrong, I in no way intend to stop caring,
But you can rest assure this shit has got to change and you
start caring.

Fuck this up if you will,
And I'm gonna give you something to feel.

Feel my heart get put on a shelf,
So, while you're trying to get feelings together,
You can do it by yourself.

So, get your feelings together and do what you need to do,
Before the only thing you are feeling is YOU!

Get Yo Shit Together

Take off your Red Dress
Put on this red robe.
Now get yo ass in the kitchen and put
Something on the stove.
Running around here acting like you got it so hard;
I can't recall the last time yo ass had a job.
Don't say it's me, 'cause I'm at work all day.
Your job with me don't start until I call and say,
"I'm on my way."

Walking around here like yo shit don't stink,
I know I bet not ever come home again to no food to eat.
You got a good man, and you don't have kids.
These other messy-ass bitches gonna make you lose,
'Cause they don't know what it's like to win.
Spending my money like it's nothing to you,
Not to mention it should be on me, and in my savings too.

Yet I support you and your dreams.
Hell, I thought we were winning; looks like we're on different
teams.
Your mouth never stops moving with all that bullshit going in
your head,
Yet you fail daily to take care of your man when it's time for
bed.
I watched you put your dreams on paper,
And how you made them sound.

*Yet it's been years now, and that shit hasn't even got off the
ground.*

*You got dreams, but can't stay out of other people's drama.
I'm confused; are you my woman or all these other
motherfuckers' mama?
If you took care of your house with the same attention,
None of this shit I would have to mention.
What about my dreams I put aside for you?
Do you have any idea all the shit that I could do?*

*I should have just walked away when your ass started to
change;
Then I forgot, my dumb ass changed your last name.
So, get your shit together, and put all this bullshit on the shelf.
Name or no name, you gone find yo ass by yourself.*

Head Game

They say what's love got to do with it, absolutely nothing.
This ain't about love; this is about straight-up fucking.
So bring that shit on and don't hold back,
You don't have time for unwinding or getting relaxed.
I'm not that one to be holding shit up;
Like I said, this ain't about love; it's time to fuck.

I see your body shaking; baby, are you scared?
You better get yo shit together; it's time for some head.
You think this a game? You better think twice;
The way my head game is, trust me, it ain't nothing nice.
My head game reaches to the depths of your soul,
I mean head, shoulders, knees and toes,
Assholes and elbows.

Keep acting like you think fat meat ain't greasy;
It's about to go down, and I won't take it easy.
One lick, two licks, three licks, four,
Eyes rolling back in your head, screaming for more.
Toes curled, back arched, palms starting to sweat,
Grabbing me by my head, saying, "Damn baby, you ain't
finished yet?"

I told you from the start, what's love got to do with it?
Just lay yo ass back; hell, I'm just beginning.
Your body desires pleasure, with just a little bit of pain;

This ain't about fucking just yet; just maintaining this head game.
True to my passion, crafty all the same,
"Whose is this?" you're screaming,
"Oh shit baby, I forgot your damn name."

"Hell, what's my name?" Even that I don't remember,
'Cause my body is shaking and trembling.
I've had head before, but this damn show ain't the same.
I see now you're starting to understand my head game.

I Do

Not all Roses are Red, nor Violets are Blue,
Nor will anyone love you the way I do.
Not all days are filled with sunshine and clouds that are blue;
There will be rainy days; you can bet that it is true.

Grass is not always green; it has browning days,
It changes with the seasons, as we do with our ways.
All water is not hot, nor even cold;
Sometimes the water is just water that chills and warms our
soul.

All blood is not the same, or our DNA;
There's A, B, AB, and O, Positive and Negative,
Yet it all leaks the same way.

One thing's for sure: Roses, Violets red or blue,
Rain, Grass with seasons changed,
Hot, Cold, Warm with chills,
DNA or Blood, it's all just the same.

It doesn't matter what it do;
I do, I do, I do love you.

I Give Up

I give and I give, but all you do is take,
All you care about is you, but not how my heart aches.
I strive for perfection to make you see me,
Always trying to be what you want me to be.
Still, all you seem to care about is you, not me.

Pushing myself to limits beyond myself,
Steady watching myself getting dusty on the shelf.
One that I tried to get off of just to show you it's you that I
need,
But I'm fucking tired of always saying please,
Getting down on my knees, developing scars, and can't
breathe,
Suffocating even in my dreams,
Yet you still don't see who I am, so it seems.

Always for you, never against;
My heart is breaking; this shit is too intense.
Wondering in my mind what the fuck did I miss.
Always picturing how it is supposed to be,
Lost in the shadows of what used to be me.
The Person, The Myth, The Unselfish One who gives and loves
unconditionally.
Yeah, yeah, yeah, that was me.

Now I lay with tears in my eyes,

Being battered blow by blow, surprise by surprise.
Tears so hard I can hardly open my eyes,
Yet bracing myself for yet another surprise,
But not surprised 'cause it seems like the norm.
Yet you don't see the inside of me and what you've harmed.

Shattered but not fully broken, deep cracks maybe one or
two,
Still trying all that is within me just to continue to love you.
Doing all that I can to show you my heart is true.
Never remembering all you care about is you.

I give and I give, and that part of me really sucks;
Not much left of this me, so it's about time for this me to give
the fuck up.
Change me? No, just shower me,
Wash myself off to be who I used to be.
Once again going back to loving me,
Opening my eyes so I can see all the love that's inside of me.

One will never understand how much is given until it's gone,
One will never see it 'cause they see nothing wrong.
Continue to give 'cause that's who you be;
Just make yourself your priority.

I Missed You

I didn't want to tell you that I missed you 'cause
I didn't want you to see me cry.
My heart was beating so fast when I saw you,
And I kept asking myself why.

I've seen you before in various ways,
But today I felt like I was in a daze.
I came just to give you a hug,
But what I really wanted was to feel your love.

I dreamed about you last night, and I woke up
With you on my mind.
I knew no matter what, today I had to make
Some time.

Time to see you and tell you I love you,
But when I saw you, I didn't know what to do.
I grabbed you and pulled you tight;
I wanted to squeeze you with all my might.

Yet it was gentle, soft, and sweet;
If I weren't holding you, I would have fell
Off my feet, 'cause my knees were so weak.

As I watched you walk away,

A slight tear came down.
I quickly wiped it away so it would not be shown.

As I drove off, your smile became mine;
It was like my face was suspended in time.
All I know is I missed you,
Then when you grabbed me and laid your head on my chest,
I felt how much you missed me too.

I Need

I need a pussy to eat,
One that can make me weak.
I need a woman to please,
One that can knock me to my knees.

I need some toes to suck
And a woman who loves to fuck,
One who is not some bullshit, 4 or 5 times a month;
I need a freak,
One who knows how to put my ass to sleep.

Wake me up to the sounds so sweet,
Then the warm feel of her lips all over me,
A woman who's not scared to please her man,
Doing it as often as she can.

As often doesn't mean a little here or there;
As often means... hell, just about anywhere.
I need a pussy with a super hot clit,
One that my tongue can lick and flip.

One I can suck on from dusk to dawn,
One that's not afraid to gift me with all its cum,
Rubbing it on my lips and then my face,
Sticking your fingers in my mouth so I can have a good taste.

I need a pussy that will love for me to make it cum.
Tell me, baby, is your pussy the one?

35

I Never Knew

I never knew I could love someone, then my eyes caught a
glimpse of you.
I never knew love would affect me the way you loving me do.
I never knew what real love was 'til I saw your smile;
I never knew how love really felt until the day you drove me
wild.

I never knew you could taste love until my lips met yours;
I never knew how bright love was until I saw stars shining all
over you like the stars above.
I never knew I could swallow love until the moment I
swallowed you.
I never knew I could feel love running through my veins;
I never knew love could change me until I found out your
name.

I never knew love could make you give a part of you that you
never knew you had.
I never knew love could make you smile at the thought of love
even when you're mad.
I never knew love could make you feel the pain of another,
especially when they're sad.
I never knew I could love the way I do;
I never knew what love was 'til the moment I laid eyes on
you.

I Want You

I want you; I want to kiss your lips.
I want to rub and squeeze your ass and grip your hips with
my fingertips.
I want to hold you close and look into your eyes,
Want to slowly run my hands up and down your thighs.

I want to taste you and consume you from your head to your
feet;
Girl, just thinking about you makes me weak.
I want to grab you, pull you by your hand;
I want you to feel how deep my love for you spans.

I want you like the water needs the sea;
I want you. Now the question is, do you want me?

I Was Thinking

I was thinking of you, and why I don't know;
For some reason, I want to fuck you all over the floor.
I was wondering, for some reason, why I felt that way;
Hell, I discovered it was just one of the ways I think about
you each day.

So many things come across my mind;
When I think about you, my mind gets suspended in time.
For some reason, I can picture your eyes looking into mine;
Then I discover, too, at that time, your mind is also
suspended in time.

So far gone that it seems there is no way back;
So far gone, looking like a motherfucker on crack.
Glassy eyes, mind just gone;
You could be at your front door and still be thinking you're
not home.

It's amazing just how good something could be—
Something special, even magical, it seems.
Running your ass home just to get that pussy ready,
Candles burning, music playing, waiting to hit the bed.

Oh shit, we still haven't made it to the bed;
Just a few strokes to put you to sleep.

Damn, I forgot how just a few strokes make you weak.
That's what I think about when I think about how good it
could have been between you and me,
Having your ass glowing like a bright-ass sunbeam.

To grind on me like I like it, slow and steady,
Waiting on me, standing by the door,
Waiting for me to ravish that pussy, then you giving me some
amazing head.
I was thinking about you, and why I don't know;
For every moment I think about you,
My fucking feelings start to grow.

I Will Never Forget

I will never forget the day that I met you;
I told you how beautiful you were, how fine you were.
You looked into my eyes and said I better respect you.

I watched you walk with such elegance and grace,
Wondering in my mind how good you would taste.
I could smell your scent like flowers and rain;
I knew then I wanted to change your last name.

I followed you like a dog in heat,
Ready to consume you like a piece of fresh meat.
Saying in my mind, "This will take time,
Working on my game plan, 'cause you had to be mine."

Saying to myself, "God, this bet not be a test,
But if it is, let my words be my best."
I'll never forget the day that I met you;
Give me the tools to get her to say yes,
To just one date, and I will do the rest.

I think back to that day; it's still fresh like the morning dew—
Captivating, exquisite, and a smile that said so much.
I didn't care what it took; I had to feel your touch.

I will never forget the day that I met you;

If You Only Knew

If you only knew how much I care for you,
If you only knew how much I love you,
If you only knew the things that you do
When you do what you do that makes my heart turn sunshine
blue.

If you only knew how I cry for you,
If you only knew how I wake up hoping
Just to see a picture of you
To make the dream that I just had come true.

If you only knew the way I get when you talk,
And OMG, how I get watching you walk.
If you only knew the thoughts that go through my mind,
Wishing and praying that your thoughts are the same as
mine.

I know you detached, but yo ass got me out here feigning
Like I'm on crack.
If you only knew how much I desire you—
OMG, I wish.

If you only knew.

I'm Fucked

I've pushed and pushed to find real love;
Then I found yo ass, and I'm falling like a wounded dove.
My heart was beating normal, then yo ass took it over;
Now it's all broken and swollen.

My head was in the right place,
Now thoughts of you have invaded all my space.
I look into the sky at night,
Watching the stars that shine so bright.
Then I look at pictures of you and cry
Until I no longer see any light.

I cry until my eyes are about to bust;
I keep telling them to calm the fuck down,
But just like my heart, they no longer trust.
I pour out my heart to yo ass like a glass of Kool-Aid,
Then thinking every day my ass is just waiting on a trade.

Get traded in like a broke-down piece of junk.
Head fucked up, heart fucked up, now something nobody
wants.
It's a miracle that I survive each day;
Hell, especially when I know shit ain't gonna go my way.

Pushing and clawing to stay afloat,

Hell, just trying my best not to choke.
Thirsty and hungry with nothing to eat or drink;
It's yo ass I want to consume, and this fucking shit is making me weak.

Man, what the fuck is a motherfucker supposed to do
When all the fuck this motherfucker does is think and dream of you?
Yeah, it's fucked up, I tell you;
Just fucked up in so many ways.
This fucking feeling won't stop, and this shit goes on for days—
Weeks and months to be exact.

Frustrated, mad, and pissed the fuck off;
Wanting to scream, but won't shit come out my mouth.
I hate this shit; I promise I do.
Wanting to love myself, but I'm too fucking in love with you.

I just quit myself for myself to love you
In spite of myself so that your love would shine bright like on a shelf.
So here's to yo ass; you got
This fucker right where you wanna.

Oh, but I ain't worried 'cause yo ass too busy running—
Running like a track star from this man with a long thick tongue.
Yeah, I said it; it got yo ass on the run.

Run on, baby, work hard and get your hustle on.
The music is starting to change;
The beat of the heart is losing range.
Singing and shouting the way I do;
The song that I sing is all about you.

Imagination Gone Wild

You walk in the room, and I see you looking all good;
I'd rip your clothes off—oh, how I wish I could.
I see you take your shirt off,
Your pants one leg at a time.
I'm screaming inside with anticipation,
Then you taking off your bra catches my eye.
Oh, wow, down comes your panties, and I can't take my eyes
off your thighs.

I see you reach for me, and my nerves begin to take hold;
I'm loving the way you're doing it; seems you're in control.
I brace myself for a moment, a pause it may seem;
I must find some way to wake up; this must be a freaking
dream.

You slowly remove my shirt, one arm at a time,
Then whisper in my ear, "Today, Daddy, you're all mine."
Then come the shoes, just slung off my feet;
Holding on to my body, from your hands I can feel the heat.

Then comes the belt, and the button is undone;
Girl, if you don't hurry up, I'm going to explode;
Yeah, that means I'ma cum.
Sliding them down slowly until I'm exposed,
Making my dick suddenly disappear;
I look down, and all I can see is your nose.

Stroking me with your lips, and oh my, that tongue;
I knew I was in trouble 'cause it was two of us—
Now we look like one.
You lay back on the bed and pull me to you;
You lay me down and start again.

All I see is your sexy stomach and those beautiful twins;
I don't know whether to scream or just get up and run.
Oh, shit, it feels so good; it feels like I'm about to cum.
You suddenly stop, and with one quick move of grace,
You land like a gymnast right on my face.

Your body already somewhat shaking as you grab to get a
grip;
I reach for you yet don't feel you until you put my hands on
your hips.
I feel you grab my head,
Your knees planted firmly into the bed.
Your body starts to go, go, go;
That hot cum starts to flow, flow, flow—
Running down my tongue, then onto my face.
I can't believe how much is coming out as your body begins to
shake.

Shaking even harder as I take my grip on your clit,
Sucking with more of a purpose as I take a tighter grip.
Up and down my tongue did go,
Then in and out of your sweet pussy hole.

I find myself quickly turning you around so I can
Lick it from behind;
What the fuck just happened? On my dick, your
Lips begin to grind.

My tongue inside your pussy and my dick inside your mouth;
I'm losing control; you're losing control, and we both begin to
shake.
This shit is about to be unreal, like a massive earthquake.
Now it's time to change things up,
But just one last kiss on the cheeks of your butt.
I pull you on top of me, and you start to grind;
Girl, you know how I love that; my mind is now suspended in
time.

Your nipples you place inside my mouth for me to taste;
I want to grip them, but I can't get my hands off your waist.
You grinding, I'm sucking; baby, it's time for some slow-
stroking loving.
I lay you on your back; you open your legs.
Once more I bury my face in your pussy, and
You once again grab my head.

You tell how much you love it over and over again;
As I look up at you, I can see you squeezing and licking on
those twins.
You call out to me, saying, "Daddy, I'm about to explode!"
Oh, shit, Daddy, this gon' be a heavy load.
"Daddy, please slide that dick inside of me quick;
I want to cum all over your dick."

Slowly we make love, embracing every stroke;
My mouth is so dry, I can't feel my throat.
I'm sweating so hard as I'm loving on you;
My dick is getting hotter; I don't know what to do.
You grab me and begin to stroke with me—
The power of our orgasms together damn near knocks me off
my feet.

I'm shaking; you're shaking; there seems to be no end.
I look at you, and you look at me;
We both speak at the same time with the same statement:
"When can we do this AGAIN?!"

It's All About That GTA

He was playing his game; I walked up and asked him for
something I could borrow.
He looked at me and said, "What?"
I grabbed his dick and said, "This is a Grand Theft Auto."

"Naw, keep playing your game; I don't need your help.
I can suck the skin off this dick all by myself."
I heard a siren sound like a major police chase,
Man, the look on this brother's face.

Up and down around the head I did go,
Pulled back a little; didn't want his ass to blow.
Heard another loud sound; his ass done dropped his remote.
I picked it up for him and gave it back,
"You're in the middle of a mission, baby; finish that contract."

Money out there to be made, properties to buy;
He could tell I wasn't gonna stop by the look in my eye.
I went down with a quickness, taking in all that I could;
I felt it start to twitch; I said, "I wish yo ass would."

Just a few more strokes, baby, just a few more;
I went all the way down this time; boom, again the remote hit
the floor.
I paused for a moment; "Babe, are you okay?"

No word, just an expression was sent my way.

I went back to work, putting more pressure than before;
Boom, it was him this time that hit the floor.
I looked at him with a big ole smile;
"Let me let you take a break for a little while."

He looked back only with a smile.
I said to him, "This was just my lips;
If you can't handle them right now, you sure can't handle
these hips."

Next time I ask you if there's something I could borrow,
Stop what you're doing, baby;
It's a Grand Theft Auto!

It Doesn't Matter

It doesn't matter if I love you or how I really feel;
It doesn't matter if every time you pass by me, it gives me
chills.
It doesn't matter if I cry just at the thought of you;
It doesn't matter how I feel 'cause you'll never understand
like I do.

It doesn't matter how I crave your touch;
It doesn't matter how I want you so much.
It doesn't matter if I need you more than you need me;
It doesn't matter; even at the thought of you now, it's making
me weak.

It doesn't matter if I'm making this rhyme;
I think over and over and over about our first time.
It doesn't matter that it's you I love to kiss;
It doesn't matter that it's not yours, but rather my wish.

It doesn't matter how I dream about you;
It doesn't matter that I do it all night, then in the daytime too.
It doesn't matter that even now my tears are starting to fall;
It doesn't matter the way I feel about you has me bouncing off
the wall.

It doesn't matter even with all my reactions;

It doesn't matter how I'm a total disaster.
It doesn't matter that you don't/didn't know;
It doesn't matter, but it does show.

It doesn't matter how your brain seems to scatter;
It doesn't matter; it just doesn't matter.

It's Bad

Is it bad to say I want to eat your pussy
Without all the sex and fucking with a lot of pushing?

Is it bad to say that I just want to lean in and smell,
Eat all I can and sell the rest like Blue Bell?

Is it bad to say that I want to suck on your toes,
Eat your pussy till your hair turns into an afro?

Is it bad to say that I want to suck on your twins,
Swallow all I can, then play on the nipples in the end?

Is it bad to say that I'm thinking this way,
Knowing good and well I could fuck you every day?

Is it bad to say that my dick is hard
While I'm sitting here thinking about eating your pussy—
man, this is like a job?

Is it bad to say that I think about it all the time?
Just the thought of eating your pussy has
Me losing my mind.

Just Hoping

I hope your day is going well;
Mine is not 'cause your scent I didn't get to smell.

I hope you are having withdrawals too,
Maybe missing me the way I miss you.

I hope your heart is sort of skipping a beat,
Wishing and hoping it could be close to me.

I hope your tongue feels like you are about to choke,
Wishing it could try and go down my throat.

I hope your feet are so hot with heat,
Wishing they could get a good massage and a licking from
me.

I hope your stomach does not follow your plan,
'Cause it yearns for the touch of my warm hands.

I hope you seriously think about me sometime today,
Without just thinking about me and saying, "Okay."

I hope you understand why I do what I do;

*It's 'cause I'm always—I mean constantly—thinking about
you.*

*I see your smile, and I know what you are gonna say,
So I'll say it for you... "Okay."*

Lost & Confused

Mouthwatering, body still throbbing;
Wish it would stop, but it's just getting harder.
Mind blown, don't know what to do with myself;
Please, somebody help me get off this shelf.

Stuck in a place I've never been,
My whole body is shaking; when will this shit end?
Had my share, and some were just a snack;
Karma really is a motherfucker,
'Cause this shit is like crack.

So paranoid, I can hardly see,
Got me so fucked up, I'm climbing trees just to pee.
Somebody help me, my head's starting to spin;
Help me, help me; when will this shit end?

I found a mirror; it was hard to see;
No way the person I see was me.
Lost within myself, afraid to leave from within;
Somebody please help me—again, when will this shit end?

Love Motion

Loving someone has never been more easy than me loving
you;
If it wasn't for all the saved memories, I don't know what I
would do.
I used to beg you for more memories so I could
Just look at you all the time,
Just knowing a small part of you was mine.

I see you, and I smile;
I mean I smile for a while.
You're the kinda woman that could possibly make a brother
go wild.
You're beautiful to me even when you don't think you are;
Just FYI, you are my bright and shining star.

Yes, I'm into you; I have to admit,
But the spell you had on me was some powerful shit.
From the soles of your feet to your wild-ass hair,
I used to want to make love to you any damn where.

Any place on earth, as long as I could feel your body against
mine,
I would be literally lost; I mean lost in time.
I can just see your body moving and the motion of your hips,
Then feel the warmth of your mouth on my dick with the
motion of your lips.

I can feel you sucking me and stroking me at the same time;
I can feel myself starting to scream as you climb up on me
and start to just slow grind.
No putting it in, just grinding up and down,
Driving your own self crazy,
Ready to lay on your back and let this tongue put it down.

I can see myself pleasing you in each and every way;
I don't know what to do 'cause I want and need to please you
every day.
I want to kiss and lick your stomach, sliding my tongue up
and down,
Kissing your navel, making my tongue go round and round.

Just listening to all those sexy, freaky, seductive sounds.
Just know loving someone has never been easier,
As much as the way I love you.

Loving You

Loving you and loving you from way beyond my means,
Thinking that loving you could fulfill all your dreams.

Loving you and loving you until my mind is frozen like ice,
Then looking in the mirror and discovering,
Looking at myself, it's me I'm starting to dislike.

Loving you and loving you; how can I make your dreams
come true?
When all my dreams have been put aside in place of loving
you.

Loving you and loving you is so not easy to do,
Yet I find new ways each day of falling in love with you.

Loving you and loving you seems like the same old song,
Especially when loving you, I'll never know what's right,
When I'm always wrong.

Loving you and loving you is a job within itself,
Loving you and loving you has caused a blow to my health.

Loving you and loving you has my spirit so weak,
Loving you makes my stomach meet my lips,
So it's hard for me to eat.

Loving you and loving you, yet hard, but easy to do;
Loving you and loving you can't go on until I learn to love me
too.

61

12 Play

You climbing up on my face.
Me stopping you so I can say my grace.

Good bread, good meat,
Good gosh, let's eat.

Licking you all over from your head to your feet.
Playing with each hair on your legs like a smooth jazz player,
Searching for every sweet and delicious flavor.

Crying out in silence just wishing you would know
How I'm gonna fuck you until your hair turns into an Afro.

It may take only once or a few times in between,
But I'm a man on a mission and you know what that means.

Yes, fucking you until you shout,
Then licking that pussy 'til you pass the fuck out.

Not tapping out and quitting like you have done,
But passing out completely so I know I have won.

So come on baby and climb up on this face,

I'll pause for one moment just to say my grace.

Then it's me, you,

Yes baby, it's about to be a 12 Play.

My Dreams

Sun shining bright as it may seem,
You're the one that has been running around in my dreams.

Poking and touching for things to do,
Getting me all worked up, just so I can fuck you.

Keep playing around, and I'ma tap that ass,
Have you whining like an ATM that's out of cash.

Playing with me is not your best choice;
Your ass gonna fool around and lose your heart.
Once it's gone, I'm playing for keeps,
Finding every angle to make your ass weak.

This is not a game; if it is, you shouldn't play,
Waking me up at night will get you fucked all day.
You think you're fine and sexy; it's true,
You haven't experienced half the shit I will do to you.

Things may not always be as they seem;
I bet you'll think twice before you come back into my dreams.

My Garden Flower

You're like a rose from your head to your toes;
Just the smell of you brings a calm within my soul.

Your grace, the way you flow as you walk,
The sweet smell of the simplicity of things I get just by
hearing you talk.

The glow on your face, just like the morning dew;
Although I love your smell, I just can't stop looking at you.

I would love to see you in bunches, or maybe a pair of two,
So I can keep one for myself and then give the other back to
you.

I've seen you as the wind begins to blow,
Your body moving oh so gently; it has a sway of its own.

You're something the whole world needs to see,
So I dare not keep you captive just for me.

So I'll share you with them all and watch you soar in the
breeze;
I know just like me, you too have needs.

Blossom, blossom, my sweet rose;
Where you will end up, nobody knows.

But for now, just know all I see is you;
You're not just something out of my dreams,
You're my dream come true.

My Hated Desire

Seeing you and wanting you sets my soul on fire;
Loving you and being with you is my heart's desire.

I can't imagine loving someone the way I could love you,
Yet finding out your true story is one that is so untrue.

I've been through the rain and the storm with so many
others;
I'm damn sure not gonna do this shit with you.

I tried to understand why things seem so hard for you to
understand;
That's what's wrong with people—they don't know when they
got gold in their hand.

I can't tell you how many times I cried over you,
Not just you, but the bullshit you say and do.

Playing with people's hearts with no notion,
Fucking all that you can with no emotion.

Taking in all that you can, yet you want me to be your man;
I don't do tricks that treat,
You thinking about me while sucking another dude's meat.

Playing fucked-up games gonna get that ass slowly let down six feet.
I could love you 'cause you set my soul on fire,
But the way you are, you will just be my hated desire.

My Morning

I woke up to the sound of thunder and rain,
Yet all I could feel was hurt and pain.
I tried and tried to get things off my mind;
I knew I had to try harder, and it would take time.

As the drops became harder and things seemed so unreal,
With thoughts on my mind, I could not hold back my tears.
They fell out of my eyes like the pouring rain;
The more they fell, the more I felt pain.

Thunder then lightning, winds soaring with such force;
The walls were closing in around me,
While outside, nature was taking its course.

I screamed, I yelled as if someone could hear me;
Then I realized there was no one near me.
I screamed, I cried; I was in shock and fear.
They came harder now, stronger now, one tear after tear.

Bursting through my tear ducts at a steady stream,
They began to fall harder than the rain, it seemed.
They stopped—yes, they stopped with no warning or
anything;
I woke up; it was pouring, but my tears were just a dream.

My Thoughts From Within

I'm forever changing, day by day;
From love to hurt, then feeling some type of way.

One day I don't care about the world;
The next I do.
One day I want to cuddle;
The next just simply, "Fuck you."

I've been through so much, ups and downs,
High as the sky, lower than the ground.
I've been spun around, blown like a tree in the wind;
It's easy to say, here are my thoughts from within.

Moments in life make or break us,
Trials we sometimes overcome,
Journeys sometimes evade us,
Many victories we haven't even won.

Sometimes we are so afraid
That one day we may finally win,
That we forget to verbalize our thoughts from within.

So today it changes; today it becomes brand new;
Today this is all about me and you.
Things you wish you would have said, but I do.

Your inner feelings, your bold mind,
Your heart, your time,
Your soul and your body,
Being in love, then being a little naughty.

Take a moment so now we both can win;
Welcome to my thoughts from within.

My Wants

I want to taste your lips,
Grip your hips,
Go up and down your ass with my fingertips.

Taste your lips below your hips;
Let my tongue go up and down, round and round on your
nipples at the tip.

Taste your neck, both sides,
Rotating back and forth until I make you close your eyes.
Letting my hands go up and down your sexy thighs,
Tasting your tongue on the tips of my lips.

Followed by the grind of your demanding hips,
Demanding for my grip.
The more I grip your hips,
The more you push your tongue deeper in between my lips.

Begging me to suck it with a light but sensuous stroke,
Causing you to lose your breath
As I pull it further down my throat.

I want to please you, baby, like never before,
Have you naked and waiting for me, spread eagle on the bed
or the floor.

I want to please you, baby, from head to toe;
Girl, you already know how this tongue works—
Turns perms back into an afro.

I want to please you, baby, like water needs grass;
Head, shoulders, knees, toes, and oh yes, I won't forget that
ass.
I want to please you, baby, like no man has ever done;
Make you tap out, declaring me the winner, screaming,
"Daddy, you won!"

I want to taste you, lick you, yes, and make you scream;
I want to please you so damn good, baby;
I want you to feel me pleasing for days later, even in your
dreams.

Need A Woman

I need a woman that for no reason
Would treat me like a king,
Always staring at me like I'm a big ole diamond ring.

Writing my name in her notebook like we used to back in
school,
A woman who knows her place and knows how to play by the
rules.
A woman who's not afraid to speak her mind,
A woman who knows not to be tripping but rather to value
our time.

To accept her feelings and embrace them at the same time,
Not caring what the situation is; when we're together, I'm
hers, she's mine.
Knowing it may not be often that the two of us can meet,
Yet searching daily to find ways that will make each other
weak.

Not afraid to tease when we are not close,
Having me climb a wall or two as I watch you up close,
Almost as if I could touch you, as if we were in the same
home,
Doing things that would make me lick my own damn phone.

I need a woman who's good with her hands,
Not afraid to take charge and show me I'm her man.
I need a woman who's not afraid to pin me against the wall,
Holding on tight to my knees as she does some thangs to me
so that
I don't fall.

I need a woman that's not scared to please me in the car;
Tinted windows or not, a drive near or far.
A woman who will wake up just to take a pee,
Then climb back in the bed and begin to suck on me.

I need a woman that will walk past me on the couch,
Stop just for a moment and put her nipple in my mouth.
Take my hand and place it between her thighs,
Whisper in my ear and tell me, "This pussy is all mine."

Not afraid to fuck at the drop of a dime,
Not afraid to feed me that pussy,
Not afraid to ride my face from time to time.

I want a woman who's not afraid for me to pull her hair,
A woman who will fuck me anywhere.
A woman who will grab me by my head
And tell me to eat her pussy from the floor to the bed.

Call me Daddy and tell me to eat her pussy till she gets weak;
The kitchen counter, the bathroom sink.

A woman who will cook for me even when I don't ask,
Not just because I just finished spanking that ass.

A woman who will buy all the food and drinks,
Then have me in the kitchen cooking and busting my ass over
the sink.
A woman who is confident in her shape and size,
A woman who will do whatever it takes to roll back my eyes.

A woman who is independent and has her own,
But knows how to respect the fact that when I'm there, it's our
home.
A woman that does all that she can;
No worries, 'cause if she's all of that woman, I'll be just as
much man.

Nice not Nice

Hello baby, how you been?
It's nice to see your face again!

I remember when you were around,
But then it's funny how you put me down.
I was so much into you;
Remember all the things we used to do?

Remember how things were okay?
You thought you could do better, so you went on your way.
You thought what we had was so untrue,
But for me, all I thought of was you.

I spent so many years chasing after you;
All I got was my feelings turned blue.
I wiped my tears and said that it's okay;
I picked myself up and went on my way.

You'd pop up from time to time,
Then there I go again, wishing you were mine.
You call, and I fall;
We talk for days, then when I call, you don't answer,
And I find myself beating my head against the wall.

You act like you want me, and I have wanted you for so long;

Then it winds up being the same old sad song.
What is it with you?
You know how I feel; my feelings have always been true for
you.

I didn't care if you were with someone else;
Just tell me the truth so I don't feel like I hate myself.
For just sitting and waiting for you like I always do,
Then once again, the hurt begins to come through.

You with someone else or even me too;
I didn't care as long as I could express my love and feelings to
you.
You kick me to the curb, then expect me to respond to you
When you text or call.
Really? To what? Get my feelings hurt once again through it
all?

Knowing I have truly loved you this long,
My heart is no joke, in which you may think.
I don't want to face disappointment once again,
And I know I would.
That's why I feel like I feel now...
LOVE STINKS!!!!!!!!!

So forgive me for not responding the way you think I should;
Just hearing your voice or seeing a picture of you
Would knock me off a cliff, as they always do.
So don't tell me you get the message

When I haven't heard from you in months, maybe even a year
nearly.

I hope all is well and you are okay;
I hope things in your life are going your way.
So hello baby, how you been?
It was nice to hear from you again.

Pleasure And Pain

You say you like pleasure with just a little bit of pain;
Just FYI, my tongue is longer and bigger than most men's
dick game.
You say you want to be totally satisfied;
Well, lay yo ass back and close your motherfucking eyes.

Yeah, don't look; there won't be no delay;
Your mind should be ready for takeoff, like a plane on a
runway.
Inside of you I will go, slowly seeking that spot;
Don't push back, baby, 'cause when I hit it, trust I won't stop.

Not until I spank that ass a little for a slight bit of pain;
Not even when you are yelling out my name.
Not until I make that pussy rain.
You say you like pleasure with just a little bit of pain;
Well, don't trip, baby, when you call your pussy by my name.

In and out till the faucet turns off,
Then I'll take that hot clit deep inside my mouth,
Gently sucking it in a motion you can't understand,
Screaming, "Let it go," trying to move my hands.

Naw baby, this is what you dreamed of;
So close your eyes; here come the stars above.

Close your eyes and whisper my name;
Yes baby, here comes the rain.

Over and over, time after time;
No worries for right now; it's mine.
I'll give it back as soon as I'm done,
Not before your pussy and my tongue truly become one.

All pleasure and a little bit of pain;
After this moment, you will never forget my name.

Pressure

Bow my head and close my eyes;
Right before my face enters between your thighs.
I was raised correctly, so I eat with a pace,
But before I eat, I must say my grace.

Good bread, good meat, good gosh, let's eat;
Head, shoulders, knees and toes,
Assholes and elbows.
I'm slow at first with good intentions,
Then things get going a little faster;
Hold on tight 'cause I'm on a mission.

Poised for the long haul, ready for my surprise,
Searching for that creamy creation,
Bracing so you won't squirt in my eyes.
Longer strokes now, from your clit to your hole,
Hesitating for a moment—oops, inside I go.

On the edge for a second, then inside and deep;
I see your back starting to arch as on my back go your feet.
I look up to see you, and all I see is your chin,
As I reach up to squeeze those beautiful twins.

Back down I go, inside as well;
Not one second goes by before I hear you scream, "Oh hell!"

Then comes the explosion, the first of many;
Now you know why they call me Mr. Good and Plenty.

It's not long before explosion number two;
"Damn baby, you yell, what the fuck am I going to do with
you?"
"Hold on baby, I won't be too long,
But one thing's for sure, you gonna take this tongue."

Explosion number three, followed by number four;
Bam bam, my head hits the floor.
You push me up off you, screaming, "Please let it go;
Me and my pussy can't take no more."

I ease up; I come in close,
I whisper, "Okay baby, I won't give you no more."
You look up at me and ask for some dick;
"Please baby, don't be long, for once make it quick."

I look down at you, I say, "Baby, I'm done;
You can't have this dick if you can't take this tongue."

Relatively Thinking

Girl, I fucking love you; yes, you are my trophy.
You say you love me, so show me that you're worth it.
You kill me saying I'm the man of your dreams,
Yet you keep entertaining other motherfuckers,
Trying to get you on their team.

How do I compete when I'm working hard as hell,
Trying someday to provide you with a home instead of that fucking shell?
Yeah, shit is hard, and yeah, this shit is real;
At least I'm not just fucking around; I'm trying to keep shit real.

Fucked up how someone is genuinely good to another motherfucker,
But you give that motherfucker nothing but fucking trouble.
I hear you say how you feel with me,
Especially when my ass is down on my knees.

Giving you pleasure, that good head,
When all I could care about is my nut instead.
Sending your ass to the moon and back,
Licking your ass from head to toe, including your ass crack.

Yeah, I said it, and I'm not ashamed;

I do what I do because I want to change your damn last
name.
You said it yourself and made me believe it's true;
Ain't no other motherfucker can do you like I do.

You think it's a game, baby, just walk out the gate;
When you get with that other motherfucker, maybe then
you'll look back and appreciate.
I said it before, and I'll say it again,
If you just handle your business constantly, shit, your ass will
win.

Don't get caught up in what you see others do;
This is about making your fucking dream come true.
Imagine getting what you get once or twice a week,
When it will be every night, your ass will be weak.

So play on if you want to and let social media run me away;
Sunshine may be in the sky,
But your life will feel like a cold and dreary day.
You have the best of me;
No patience will run away the rest of me.

Doing shit that you know ain't cool,
Making me feel like a motherfucking fool.
Testing my patience won't make shit move any faster;
Testing my patience is gonna cause a disaster.

Yes, I love you, my trophy, my queen;
Stop fucking around before I sign with another team.

Shut the Door & Turn off the Lights

Turn off the lights and close your eyes;
Let me give you what you been thinking of, surprise.
I'm feeling for you; come on and feel for me too.
Touch my hand and pull yourself in,
You been thinking about me; I've been thinking about you.

Now let's start this thing off right,
So turn off the lights.
Turn off the lights and reach for me,
Come closer and closer; let the two of us blend.

Deep in thought, breathing a little harder,
I hear it in your voice when you hear mine;
Sounds like your whole body is suspended in time.
Sounds like when I look at you, I lose my mind.

I sense in my mind you thinking of me,
Wanting to just shut the door and make me drop to my knees.
Turn off the lights and have me begging, "Baby please."
It's okay 'cause I feel the same way too,
So shut the door, turn off the lights, and see what we can
make it do.

Turn off the lights and let's get it started.

Strung Out

Mouth watering, body still throbbing,
Wish it would stop, but it's just getting harder.

Mind blown, don't know what to do with myself—
Please, somebody help me get off this shelf.

Stuck in a place that I've never been,
My whole body is shaking—when will this shit end?

Had my share, and some were just a snack,
Karma really is a motherfucker,
'Cause this shit is like crack.

So paranoid, I can hardly see,
Got me so fucked up, I'm climbing trees just to pee.

Somebody help me—my head's starting to spin,
Help me, help me, when will this shit end?

I found a mirror, I glanced to take a look,
Who would have guessed I'd be hung out on a hook.

Lost within myself, afraid to leave from within—
Somebody please help me, again, when will this shit end?

Stuck on You

I'm tripping, I can't breathe, and I got pains in my chest.
I can't sleep, I can't eat, and my body can't rest.

There has to be something for me to do,
'Cause I'm stuck on stupid, I'm stuck on you.

This drama that I'm feeling has me in civil unrest,
The torture I'm going through has to be a test.

My days are filled with ways to impress you,
My nights are filled with ways to undress you.

Emotional roller-coaster, ups and downs, rounds and rounds,
Stepping with a purpose, yet I feel like my feet are not on the
ground.

Giving in to the passion—or dreams, as they say,
Having to control my thoughts, being lost like a needle in the
hay.

Running so fast, waking up out of breath,
Hell, with just the thought of your touch, I wake up full of
sweat.

Day, noon, and then there's night—
With every passing second, I can't get it right.

There has to be something for me to do,
'Cause I'm stuck on stupid, I'm stuck on you.

Suspended

I woke from my sleep, laying next to him, wishing I was with you,
Losing my mind, suspended in time, not knowing what to do.

I've tried to hold back my feelings for you each night I close my eyes,
Yet I wake up ten times a night thinking of you, and I'm still not surprised.

When he tries to touch me, all I do is think of you.
You touch me in ways he never could do,
You touch me in ways that he should,
Now when he gives me that look, I say to myself, "I wish this motherfucker would."

He walks around acting like he's the shit,
Hell, a sista can't even get her pussy licked.

Just up and down, just a stroke or two—
Hell, one flick of your tongue, and I'm coming all over you.

I'm into him, I am; he's good for what he does,
But nothing can compare—nothing—when it comes to yours.

I hear your voice, and my toes curl,
I see your face, and it rocks my world.

I feel your touch, and I lose my mind,
Like I said, baby, you have me suspended in time.

This shit has got me tripping, and this shit is really deep,
Don't know what I'm gonna do, but I have got to get some
sleep.

Please, baby, can I have you before I go home? We have time,
So I can lay next to his ass smiling, 'cause I got mine,
Sleeping all night, suspended in time.

That Tongue

I wonder what it feels like to have a man with a tongue like mine,
One that will always make you cum, time after time.

A tongue that's like a freeway lane,
Up and down, in and out, sucking away misery and pain.

A tongue that will make you forget what your own damn name is,
Let alone a tongue that will make you definitely forget his.

A tongue that's not afraid to explore your ends and your outs,
One that knows how to navigate, taking it all into its mouth.

One that flicks you over the moon,
One that will have you panting and screaming like your voice has been finely tuned.

A tongue that will take your energy away,
A tongue that will have you wet every day.

A tongue that will never make you bored,
A tongue that will make you say, "Eat that pussy, baby, it's yours."

A tongue that's sweet, wet, hot, and divine—
I wonder what it feels like to have a man with a tongue like
mine.

95

The Benefit Package

I'm just an average woman, about five foot five,
Sexy in my own way.
A hardworking woman that puts it in, both night and day.

I'm not the woman that most can imagine—
A beautiful smile, small waist, and I'm toting one hell of a
wagon.
I'm good at what I do, absolutely fantastic;
I'm that one who takes your benefit package.

Not afraid to put my hands in places
And take a piece for me;
Not the kind of woman that's afraid to get down on my
knees—
Not just in private, but in places you won't expect, just to
please.

Touching him, running my nails all over his body;
I'm cute, I'm sexy, and show-nuff naughty.
Oh, and definitely the one to get the party started.
Don't be mad at me 'cause I know how to use what I got.

While you're denying him, trust me, I'm not.
I'm giving him all that he wants, needs, and desires—
I'm that benefit package that sets his body on fire.

I put on things to blow his mind,
Then send him home well-satisfied, 'cause you ain't giving
him his time.
I dress like he wants me; I'm the one who feeds him and
teases him each and every day.
I'm the woman that lets him have all of me, and tells him to
have me his way.

I'm that woman who treats him how a man wants to feel,
Being there to just rub his body when he's tired, and when
he's not, making sure he gets a thrill.
Letting him lick me from head to toe,
Jacking my hair up when he pleases me, from flat-ironed to
an afro.

I'm that woman he sends on exotic trips
Just because of the magic that comes from the movement of
my lips and hips.

I know you may not understand why he lays next to you and
he can't hack it.

You might be his woman, but now he's my benefit package.

The Rain

I woke up to the sound of thunder and rain,
Yet all I could feel was hurt and pain.
I tried and tried to get things off my mind;
I knew I had to try harder, and it would take time.

As the drops became harder and things seemed so unreal,
With thoughts on my mind, I couldn't hold back my tears.
They fell out of my eyes like the pouring rain;
The more they fell, the more I felt pain.

Thunder, then lightning, winds soaring with such force—
The walls were closing in around me, while outside, nature
was taking its course.
I screamed, I yelled, as if someone could hear me,
Then I realized there was no one near me.

I screamed, I cried; I was in shock and fear.
They came harder now, stronger now, one tear after tear,
Bursting through my tear ducts in a steady stream;
They began to fall harder than the rain, it seemed.

They stopped—yes, they stopped with no warning or
anything.
I woke up; it was pouring, but my tears were just a dream.

The Weekend

It's early in the morning, not sure what day;
I find myself waking up in an unfamiliar place.
There's a smell coming from somewhere deep within.
I walk to the door—it's coming from the kitchen.

I go back and lay down; I once again fall asleep.
I'm awakened with a soft touch—"Baby, I'll call you when it's
time to eat."

The voice says, "Sit up, I have something for you,"
It's a plate full of cantaloupe and honeydew.
It has sprinkles on it; what it is, I have no clue.
She says the name and says, "It's good, it's good for you."

I raise up to taste a few; the taste was different than before.
All I could do was think of her, and I kept going back for
more.

Then she came to get me, to tell me to put some clothes on.
It wasn't until then I discovered I was naked, still playing on
my phone.

I got dressed and made my way downstairs.
It was eggs, bacon, sausage, biscuits, and jams that smelled
like pears.

It smelled super good and tasted just the same—
It was one of those moments that made me want to change
her last name.

We didn't eat much more than a salad; I think a piece of
chicken or two.
Not too sure what else happened over the weekend, 'cause I
was so into you.

I know how it started; I know how it came to an end.
What I'm not sure about is what happened in between.

All I know, it was something I will never regret.
It was not just a weekend—
It was a weekend I will never forget.

Things Needed

I need a pussy to eat,
One that can make me weak.

I need a woman to please,
One that can knock me to my knees.

I need some toes to suck
And a woman who loves to fuck—
One who is not some bullshit 4- or 5-times a month.

I need a freak,
One who knows how to put my ass to sleep,
Wake me up to sounds so sweet,
Then the warm feel of her lips all over me.

A woman who's not scared to please her man,
Doing it as often as she can.
As often does not mean a little here or there;
As often means... hell, just about anywhere.

I need a pussy with a super-hot clit,
One that my tongue can lick and flip,
One I can suck on from dusk to dawn,
One that's not afraid to gift me with all its cum—

Rubbing it on my lips and then my face,
Sticking your fingers in my mouth so I can have
A good taste.

I need a pussy that will love for me to make it cum.
Tell me, baby, is your pussy the one?

Those Eyes

As my tongue flows over your body,
Seems you don't know what to do!

Eyes like diamonds when I'm kissing on you,
I feel you tense up, and a slight sigh or two.
You want to turn my way, but I won't let you.

I hear a cry softly from your lips,
Yet I also feel the movement from your hips.
Bending over slowly so I can kiss your ass,
Hoping you don't fall, 'cause you're melting like butter,
And would break like glass.

Slowly, I lift you up, with your back against my chest.
I feel your heartbeat, baby—
Are you starting to sweat?

Trembling in my arms as I grip your breast,
Your hands all over my head,
Anxiously anticipating what's happening next.

I turn you to face me so I can look into your eyes—
Wait, did you just run from me,
As if I'm surprised?

Bring yo' ass back here; I have a gift for you.
I know you're not ready, baby,
But let's see what this tongue can do.

Open up, baby, and spread them wide.
I need plenty of room to get this tongue inside.
Wrap your legs around my head and grip my neck real tight.
Grab hold of my head; don't worry, baby, I don't bite.

Feel how I feel for you.
Even I anticipated just how I was gonna please you.
I was amazed as usual, maybe even surprised,
What the first flick of the tongue did to your eyes.

I thought they were diamonds shining brightly through my
soul.
I looked again, and they were like dark pieces of coal,
As your body started to lose control.
Even the dark pieces captured my soul.

I had to regain my composure, had to stay in control.
You climbed up on top of me, and again, that look in your
eyes.
You wanted to say something, but you held it inside.

Suddenly, as you begin to grind,
Bingo! There goes one of five.

Your eyes were like diamonds,
Your body shivering like you were cold.
I was like the Beverly Hillbillies... I had just struck gold.

Continue to shine, my love, like you always do.
That look in your eyes is how I love to see you!

Thumb Sucker

You say your man is no longer interested in you.
Well, I'm that bitch that's doing all you won't do.

You used to be the one, his personal little toy,
Now I'm the one who gives him pure joy.

Yes, it's me—a badass bitch that's filled with trouble.
Yeah, it's me, better known as the motherfucking thumb
sucker.

Yes, I said it, and I mean that shit.
He ain't got to beg me to suck his dick.

I'll bathe him and wash it squeaky clean,
Suck it so good he even moans about me in his dreams.

True to my game, no questions asked,
I know how to make a dick get up,
Yes, and make it last.

Make it give me what I ask for at the drop of a dime.
I can fuck it like I want to, 'cause it's yours, not mine.

But keep on neglecting it, and soon you'll see trouble
When your man becomes my next thumb sucker.

I got a pussy that gets wet with the right kind of touch;
I don't give a damn about making love, I like to straight-up
fuck.

Don't confuse me for being weak;
I'm not reserved—I'm a stone-cold freak.

I'm what you wish you could be,
A badass bitch that he can't wait to see.

Five feet seven, slightly slim with big thighs,
An ass most true cowboys can't even ride.

A tongue that's long and super strong,
A sweet motherfucking pussy that can't do wrong.

A grip so tight it brings the strongest to their knees,
A fire hydrant that flows like the Mississippi, if you know
what I mean.

I'm well-versed in the language of foreplay;
I'm his Burger King, baby—he can have it any type of way.

He's not interested in you because of me.
When's the last time you dropped down on your knees?

When's the last time you laid across your bed,
Put on a beautiful smile and said, "Come give me some head"?

Put your nipple in his mouth and told him to suck this,
While reaching down and grabbing that dick—
Squeezing and stroking it, caressing his balls,
Then swallowing it until he climbs the walls.

When's the last time you bent over and spread your legs,
Then invited him to get all up in that ass?

Well, don't be mad at him; be mad at me.
I'm the one who gives him all that he needs.

I'm the one who is like no other,
I'm the one that made him my thumb sucker.

We Tripping

Girl, you better get yo' shit together,
Do what needs to be done.
Ain't no time for games, that bitch gonna think she won.

I don't want you coming crying to me,
Talking 'bout your husband is cheating on us,
When it's me he loves to eat, and you he loves to fuck.

Get a grip on that pussy and make sure it acts right,
One thing I know about him—he likes his pussy nice and
tight.

When he comes toward me, I push my finger deep into my
spot,
Then rub it across his lips while it's still nice and hot.

I love the smile it puts on his face,
Just knowing he gets to taste me every day.

Then I notice his hips move up and back,
Searching for some legs that thick dick could crack.

We better stop tripping and do what we need to do,
We gon' mess around, and it's gonna be just us two.

*"Feed me, fuck me, and leave me alone" is what he always
said.
You keep fucking him and all that shit,
And I'll keep sucking the skin off his motherfucking dick.*

*He been giving us all that he could,
Remember, he can get some pussy when he can't get no food.*

*No more tripping—let's solve this shit,
Before we lose our man to another fucking bitch.*

What am I to Do

What am I gonna do without you—cry myself to sleep?
What am I gonna do without you, 'cause I'm in way too deep?

What am I gonna do with myself when I feel lost?
What am I gonna do with myself, 'cause my heart feels
tossed?

What am I to do when I'm craving you so bad?
What am I to do when I feel less than a man?

What am I to do when I'm so in love with you?
What is it? Huh? What the fuck do I do?

What am I to do, 'cause I feel I'm in this alone?
What am I to do when I feel I am no longer strong?

What am I to do when I love you in the end?
What am I to do when you don't realize
You're not just my lover—you're quietly my best friend?

What am I gonna do without you to be able to just be me?
What am I gonna do without you? I'll just have to wait and
see.

I Need A Woman That For No Reason

Would treat me like a king,
Always staring at me like I'm a big ole diamond ring,
Writing my name in her notebook, like we used to back in
school—
A woman who knows her place and knows how to play by the
rules.

A woman who's not afraid to speak her mind,
A woman who knows not to be tripping but rather to value
our time,
To accept her feelings and embrace them at the same time,
Not caring what the situation is—when we're together, I'm
hers and she's mine.

Knowing it may not be often that the two of us can meet,
Yet searching daily to find ways that will make each other
weak.

Not afraid to tease when we are not close,
Having me climb a wall or two as I watch her up close,
Almost as if I could touch her, as if we were in the same home,
Doing things that would make me lick my own damn phone.

I need a woman who's good with her hands,
Not afraid to take charge and show me I'm her man.

I need a woman who's not afraid to pin me against the wall,
Holding tight to my knees as she does some things so I don't
fall.

I need a woman who's not scared to please me in the car—
Tinted windows or not, a drive near or far.

A woman who will wake up just to take a pee,
Then climb back in bed and begin to suck on me.

I need a woman that will walk past me on the couch,
Stop just for a moment and put her nipple in my mouth,
Take my hand and place it between her thighs,
Whisper in my ear and tell me, "This pussy is all mine."

Not afraid to fuck at the drop of a dime,
Not afraid to feed me that pussy,
Not afraid to ride my face from time to time.

I want a woman who's not afraid for me to pull her hair,
A woman who will fuck me anywhere,
A woman who will grab me by my head
And tell me to eat her pussy from the floor to the bed,
The kitchen counter, the bathroom sink—
Call me Daddy and tell me to eat her pussy 'til she gets weak.

A woman who will cook for me even when I don't ask—
Not just because I just finished spanking that ass.
A woman who will buy all the food and drinks,

*Then have me in the kitchen, cooking and busting my ass over
the sink.*

*A woman who is confident in her shape and size,
A woman who will do whatever it takes to roll back my eyes,
A woman who is independent and has her own,
But knows how to respect the fact that when I'm there, it's our
home.*

*A woman that does all that she can—
No worries, 'cause if she's all of that woman,
I'll be just as much man.*

What I Want

I want to please you and tease you,
Then I want to fuck.
I want to open up your legs and listen to your sounds,
While on your pussy, I begin to suck.

In and out my tongue will go,
What will come out, nobody knows.
Staying in one spot will not be for me—
Exploring your body will be the key.

Ravaging your body like honeybees,
While making love to both your knees.
Where my tongue goes, nobody knows,
But it will make its way down to your toes.

Treating your body with grace and class,
Just making sure I don't forget to lick your ass.

I'm horny for you, girl, can't you see?
I can't wait to feel how you decide to please me.

I want to please you and tease you, then I want to fuck.
Make sure those twins are ready,
'Cause they'll be the first to get sucked.

What Would It

What would it take for you to love?
I'm sure a miracle sent from above.

I mean a big miracle, huge it may seem—
Oh, hell, did I forget who I was talking about?
It must be a damn dream.

What would it take to be treated like your man?
Other than when you have an issue or things don't go as
planned.

When something is wrong, then funny—I'm your man.
Keep on tripping, and you're gonna lose your benefit plan.

When I Look At You

When I'm inside of you, it feels like I'm in a dream.
When you look up at me while I'm inside of you,
It puts me in a trance.

When you look down at me while you're grinding and riding
me,
It sends me to the moon.

When you look at me right before and during your release,
It's truly mesmerizing.

When I look at you after I've licked you from head to toe,
And your body has been shaking so hard—
It captivates my heart.

When I look at you after we come together,
That's the moment I see stars.

When I Think of You

Hurricanes, typhoons, winds, and rain—
Things I think of when I think of your name.

Destruction, devastation, hurt, and pain,
After a life with you, my life would never be the same.

Careless thinking, shameful smile,
Wondering when life will stop chasing me, mile after mile.

I'm tired of the thoughts that are crossing my mind,
Trapped in a maze where the sun doesn't shine.

Trapped in a whirlwind of lies and untruths,
Watching stories unfold that you told me, become untrue.

Seeing how you challenged yourself to believe it yourself,
Not caring how one would see you, just for yourself,
Just building a façade with you in mind and nothing else.

Ruthless stalker of others outside your touch,
Trying to be something you're not, so much.

Always afraid to accept who you are,

Secretly bringing others down for the rise of your star.

Hurricanes, typhoons, winds, and rain—
When I think of you, all I think of is pain.

Yes Again... Please!

You walk in the room, and I see you looking all good.
I'd rip your clothes off—oh, how I wish I could!

I see you take your shirt off, your pants one leg at a time.
I'm screaming inside with anticipation;
Then you taking off your bra catches my eye.
Oh wow, down come your panties, and I can't take my eyes
off your thighs.

I see you reach for me, and my nerves begin to take hold.
I'm loving the way you're doing it; seems you're in control.

I brace myself for a moment, a pause it may seem.
I have to find some way to wake up—this must be a freaking
dream.

You slowly remove my shirt one arm at a time,
Then whisper in my ear, "Today, Daddy, you're all mine."

Then come the shoes, just slung off my feet;
Holding onto my body, from your hands, I can feel the heat.

Then comes the belt, and the button is undone.
Girl, if you don't hurry up, I'm going to explode—yeah, that

means I'ma cum.

Sliding them down slowly until I'm exposed,
Making my dick suddenly disappear.
I look down—all I can see is your nose.

Stroking me with your lips, and oh my, that tongue!
I knew I was in trouble, 'cause it was two of us—now we look
just like one.

You lay back on the bed and pull me to you.
You lay me down and start again.

All I see is your sexy stomach and those beautiful twins.
I don't know whether to scream or just get up and run.
Oh shit, it feels so good, it feels like I'm about to cum.

You suddenly stop, and with one quick move of grace,
You land like a gymnast right on my face.

Your body already somewhat shaking as you grab to get a
grip.
I reach for you yet don't feel you until you put my hands on
your hips.

I feel you grab my head,
Your knees planted firmly into the bed.

Your body starts to go, go, go,
That hot cum starts to flow, fold, flow,
Running down my tongue, then onto my face.

I can't believe how much is coming out as your body begins to shake,
Shaking even harder as I take my grip on your clit,
Sucking with more purpose as I take a tighter grip.

Up and down my tongue did go,
Then in and out of your sweet pussy hole.

I find myself quickly turning you around so I can lick it from behind.
What the fuck just happened—on my dick, your lips begin to grind.

My tongue inside your pussy and my dick inside your mouth.
I'm losing control, you're losing control, and we both begin to shake.

This shit is about to be unreal—like a massive earthquake.

Now it's time to change things up,
But just one last kiss on the cheeks of your butt.

I pull you on top of me, and you start to grind.
Girl, you know how I love that—my mind is now suspended in
time.

Your nipples you place inside my mouth for me to taste.
I want to grip them, but I can't get my hands off your waist.

You're grinding, I'm sucking, baby, it's time for some slow,
stroking loving.
I lay you on your back; you open your legs.

Once more, I bury my face on your pussy, and you once
again grab my head.
You tell me how much you love it over and over again.

As I look up at you, I can see you squeezing and licking on
those twins.
You call out to me, saying, "Daddy, I'm about to explode
again!"

"Oh shit, Daddy, this gon' be a heavy load.
Daddy, please slide that dick inside of me quick.
I want to cum all over your dick."

Slowly we make love, embracing every stroke.
My mouth is so dry, I can't feel my throat.

I'm sweating so hard as I'm loving on you.

My dick is getting hotter—I don't know what to do.

You grab me and begin to stroke with me.
The power of our orgasm together damn near knocks me off
my feet.

I'm shaking, you're shaking—there seems to be no end.
I look at you, and you look at me;
We both speak at the same time with the same statement:

"When can we do this AGAIN?!"

You Think

How can she say she loves me when I don't even love myself?
She says she's invested in me, yet she has no clue of my worth.

To say she loves me and is invested is truly bold,
Like an auction—25, 35, 45, 45, 45—her ass just got sold.

Talking all that crap, trying to get me to believe it all,
She forgot who she was dealing with...
Let me remind you, chick—my name is *Lappdog*.

So bottle all that crap up, 'cause you got me over here choking.
I wish it was one of my favorite cigars, 'cause I'd light that ass up and smoke it.

You say you want me but don't know what to do.
Do you think you know? I don't think you have a clue.

So pay attention to me, 'cause I do.

You Tripping

What the fuck is wrong with you?
You tripping with me—have you fucking
Forgot who I used to be?

I may seem easy now, but that has not always been the case.
Keep fucking with me, and I'm gonna give you a taste.

Acting like you got it made 'cause I seem easy to please—
You got me fucked up; to me, you're nothing but a tease.

Walking around, not fucking me like you should—
You gon' look up one day and wish like hell you could.

Yeah, I seem easy most of the time,
But I'll drop your ass like a bad habit at the drop of a dime.

It seems you just looking for a check,
Playing with my heart and my money—you better watch
your fucking neck.

You tripping if you think I'm gonna play this shit fair,
Might make a motherfucker snatch you by your
motherfucking hair.

Drag you into a different world in one haul,
Pulling out all your hair, slamming you up and down the wall.

Keep tripping with me, and you will see
Just how it was to be the old me.

I ain't a killa, but don't push me.
Keep fucking up, and soon you will see.

Just know, your ass better stop tripping with me.

You Wouldn't Know

You wouldn't know what to do with me if I was laying next to
you,
Holding you and caressing you, squeezing you through and
through.

Listening to you moan in your sleep from how good it feels,
Making your body weak from your head to your feet.

Thoughts rolling around like marbles, all kinds in your mind,
Trying to open your eyes, but you can't—you feel blind.

You're screaming loud, out of pleasure and pain,
Yelling and screaming, calling out my name.

"Babe, babe, what are you doing to me,"
Waking up in the middle of the night just to rub your feet,
Staring at you, watching your eyes,
Screaming so loud, trying to push it out,
Yet not a sound is coming out of your mouth.

Then the touch goes to your legs, and you turn to comply,
Still in a daze, trying to figure out why.

The touch goes to your stomach, and it stays for a while,

Up and down, up and down, moving slowly side to side.

It reaches your neck and then your head,
Not staying long, 'cause it's back to your feet so I can go to
bed.

You lay there, staring into space,
You want to close your eyes and fall back asleep,
But you can't—you can't even move,
Your body is too weak.

You want to touch me, but I'm out of your reach.
No sound, just moaning—oh my, the look on your face.

You hear a slight snore—yes, that's me, I'm asleep.
It's hard to imagine what happened in the end.

Yet like I said, you wouldn't know what to do laying next to
me,

'Cause tomorrow it's going to happen all over again.

Your Body

Your body bent over,
Pussy good and wet,
Rubbing and playing with that thang,
Making a brother sweat.

Nipples good and hard,
Pointing straight at me.
I see the string as it comes out on top of your clit,
Yelling inside, trying not to scream, "Oh shit!"

You take the string and wrap it around my tongue.
I can't help myself—I'm moaning, "Mmmm, yum."

I ask for more, and you give me just that.
I feel myself throbbing, and this dick is getting fat.
I close my eyes and make a quick approach—
Swallowing it down my throat, I look up and see your eyes.

Then I feel your body start to shake,
Then it suddenly becomes numb.

When I please you, baby,
Sticking your finger in it, pulling out a long string of
goodness,
Without any notice, I fall down on one knee,

Taking all that's coming out of that pussy.

They're staring back right into mine;
They suddenly roll, and a shift has come.
Again, very quickly, it begins to shake,
Trembling over and over, then you grab and squeeze dem twins.

I feel you're losing your mind with each lick over time,
Falling deeper and deeper, being totally mesmerized.
You want to scream—I see it all over your face.

You grab a pillow and scream into it,
Blowing a hole in the same place.

I turn you over to get a look at that ass,
Knowing I'm about to put a spit shine on it that will make it shine like glass.

I start with your toes and work my way to the top,
Consuming you like water to a mop.

I land back down right on your ass—
Oh, did I mention it's about to shine like glass?

You wave me off as if you can't take any more,
Pushing me off of you, down to the floor.

It's intense, I know,
But that's what I do—
I please all of you.

Your Facade

You think you're special, but I peeped your game.
It took me a while, but you just wanted a name change.

You thought you were playing me and figured it was cool,
Now look who's standing there, looking like a damn fool.

Time went by, and my thoughts became answers in my head.
There I was, thinking I was in love with a goddess,
But the devil was lying in my bed.

No matter how hard I pushed, how hard I strived,
All you saw were future dollar signs in your eyes.

It wasn't me you were in love with—
It turned out to be a facade, total bullshit.

Bullshit that turned into hatred and rage,
While I was pouring out my heart and putting it on stage.

You were loving the limelight and what my future could
bring,
While I was trying my best to utilize the gift I was given.
All you seemed to care about was how other people were
living,

*Trying to live beyond your means, totally forgetting this was
supposed to be a team.*

*It was my bad—you wanted to live for you; all that was my
dream.*
I didn't see the picture, you know, the scheme of things.

*You put on a great facade when all you had to do was your
job,*
Yet you planned your attack like a leader of the mob.

*When you saw that your attack had failed, you were quick to
yell I was wrong.*
You looked up, and I was yelling, "Deuces, I'm gone."

As I was leaving, I saw your eyes fill with rage.
I guess you thought all of this was staged.

I saw your facade hit the floor.
I pushed the button—down went the garage door.

I drove off, I could see again to my surprise.
No longer blind, I could see through my own eyes.

What others tried to get me to understand,
All the while, me just trying to be a man.

You thought you were special—yeah, I peeped your game.
You did, in fact, get a name change.

Now change it back; it is yours no more.
It left when I pushed the button and down went the garage
door.

Your Question

You asked me if I missed you,
Instead of just saying that you missed me.
Kinda makes you feel like it only mattered if I missed you, I
see.

I could say I missed you like I did the days before,
Yet I'm not sure it matters; I feel you don't think about me
once you walk out the door.

Yes, it shows at times, but not enough to keep my mind on
you.
I mostly feel like this is just something to do.

Yeah, I know I make your body shake, and it feels extremely
good too,
But after that is over, I'm lost, not knowing what's next to do.

Easy to love you, but hard at the same time.
I was all yours, but you were never all mine.

Yummy

Yummy, yummy, yummy.
You in that stand, me on my knees and hands,
Eating your pussy with your back against the wall,
Holding onto you tight so your ass doesn't fall.

Looking up at you as you stare into space—
If you could only see that look you have on your face.

Begging I go deeper but slow at the same time,
Letting your legs rest on my shoulders so you can make that
ass slow grind.

Pushing that pussy up higher towards the sky—
Man, that look on your face, the look don't lie.

I feel you pulsating, it's getting harder and harder with every
flick.
I can tell I'm right in that spot with every long, slow stroking
lick.

Suddenly, an eruption, and your body starts to shake.
I feel your cum, baby, my tongue is starting to bake.

It's not over, baby, as I lick off all that sweet foam.

Time for round two—welcome to the pleasure zone.

Do I Miss You

Do I miss you? Yes, I do.
What is it I miss?
Baby, it's all of you.

Do I crave you? Yes, I do.
What do I crave?
Just a touch or two.

Am I feeling you? Yes, just a little bit.
Do I think about you? Yes, the way you like talking shit.

Do I want to taste your lips? Yes, I do.
Do I want to grip your ass and rub your hips? Yes, I do.

Do I want your tongue deep down my throat?
Yes, so deep it almost makes me choke.

Am I worried about that between me and you?
No, baby, 'cause it's not about me or you—
It's about just us two.

Will it change in December? That's yet to be seen.
Will I see things differently by then? It's already in my
dreams.

Will you be able to change my mind?
Then, girl, you better get on yo' grind!

What do I see when I look into your eyes?
It's hard to tell, 'cause when I look into your eyes, all I see is
mine.

You looking at me and me looking at you,
Wondering all kinds of shit that our minds have put us
through.

So, do I miss you? Girl, yes, I do.
What is it I miss? Baby, simply put—

YOU!

My Thoughts of You

I closed my eyes and said a prayer or two.
The moment they opened, all thoughts went to you.

What are you doing?
What do you have on?
Are you thinking like I'm thinking?
Like I wish you were in my arms.

I close them again, and your figure appears.
Damn, girl, your beauty almost brings me to tears.

My body begins to ache,
My mouth becomes dry,
You're running through my mind,
My eyes start to cry.

Memories not yet made,
Stories none yet to tell,
Yet every time I see you in my dreams,
It's like I know you so well.

Growing pains continue,
Stomach all in knots,

Can't even sleep for asking myself why.

Closer you appear,
So close I can touch.
I feel my heart beating faster—
This seems like it's too much.

Then suddenly, I wake up,
Reality has taken you away.
I say to myself, "We can retry another day."

I roll over and look at the time—
It's only 1 a.m., I still have time.
You better bring yourself back into my mind.

Five more hours, and I know exactly what to do—
Settle in and continue all of my thoughts of you.

You & Me

You came out of the shower, and I immediately grabbed your hand.
I looked deeply into your eyes as I led you to the bed.

I laid you back and kissed you on the nose,
My next kiss was on the tip of your toes.

I noticed your body was glistening wet,
You had dried off, but your body was not completely dry yet.

I took your towel and slowly dried the moisture off,
Hoping there was no moisture coming from my mouth.

I rubbed your body with some warm body oil,
Looked into your eyes—"You're mine, baby, and this is how you'll be spoiled."

I rub your body down and give you an awesome massage,
Making sure to cover every spot, just listening to you make noise.

Moan after moan, moving with my motion,
I can see your eyes rolled back as I rolled you over.

As I finished your massage, your glow became a shine,
Laying there, looking like a brand-new dime.

I whisper in your ear, "Aren't you glad you're mine?"

I lay down and pull you close to me,
The scent of your body is oh so sweet.

You reach for my hand, and our fingers interlock.
My body actually jumps from the slight shock.

We talk for an hour or so, maybe even two.
You reached to hold me, but I insisted I wanted to hold you.

I turned on one of our favorite songs,
We listened as our breaths sounded deep.

I reached to touch your chest,
So I could feel your heartbeat.

You moved your body closer,
As we still lay hand in hand.
You turn towards me and whisper, "I'm so glad you are my
man."

After that, I couldn't sleep;

I watched you sleep—it was very deep.

The moment I fell asleep, I could feel your heartbeat.
You had turned towards me and laid your head on my chest.

I asked you, "What's wrong?" and you said,
"It's the only way I can rest."

You gripped me tighter; I could feel your breath.
I turned slightly; suddenly, we were chest to chest.

Then that damn alarm went off and messed up the rest.